Snow and Ice

Joy Palmer

Watts Books
London • New York • Sydney

© Watts Books
This edition 1995
Watts Books
96 Leonard Street
London EC2A 4RH

Franklin Watts Australia
14 Mars Road
Lane Cove
NSW 2060

UK ISBN: 0 7496 0643 6

Series editor: A. Patricia Sechi
Design: Shaun Barlow
Cover design: Edward Kinsey
Artwork: Kevin Wells
Cover artwork: Hugh Dixon
Picture research: Ambreen Husain

A CIP catalogue record for this book
is available from the British Library

Printed in Italy by G. Canale & C. SpA

King's Road Primary School
Rosyth - Tel: 313470

Contents

What are snow and ice?

Clouds are made of tiny droplets of water. When these freeze, they change into **ice crystals**. The crystals move around inside the cloud. They collide and stick together. When they are large enough and heavy enough, they fall out of the cloud. If the temperature is below freezing, they fall as snowflakes.

▽ As snowflakes fall on top of each other they pile up and cover the ground.

Sticking flakes

As snowflakes fall from a cold cloud, they become softer and stick together very easily. Soft flakes can be rolled into balls and used to build interesting shapes. Every snowflake has six sides. Millions of them fall, and no two are ever the same. They are all slightly different. The clouds in the sky, and the snow that falls from them, are part of the world's **water cycle**.

▷ Water moves around Earth in a never-ending cycle.

▽ Snow is a good material to build with. These shapes have been built for a snow festival in Japan.

4

▽ The air rises and cools turning the vapour back into droplets of water. This is how clouds form.

▽ Water dries up from the surface of oceans and rivers. In the air it becomes an invisible gas called water vapour.

◁ The droplets of water in the clouds freeze and fall as snow when the air is very cold.

◁ All snowflakes have six sides, but the patterns they make are different.

Ice from the sky

Sometimes hard balls of ice form inside a storm cloud. They are tossed around inside the cloud and bump into water droplets. The droplets freeze onto the balls of ice, adding extra layers of ice. When the balls are heavy enough, they fall to the ground with great force and are called hailstones. Hailstones can cause a lot of damage.

▷ Hailstones fall to the ground with great force. They are usually about the size of a pea, but they can be as large as a melon!

◁ These crops have been ruined by hailstones.

▽ A hailstone is made of several layers of ice.

Frost

During the night, when the sun does not shine, the ground cools down. In winter the **temperature** may fall below **freezing point**. If the night air contains a lot of moisture, the invisible droplets of water will freeze when they meet something very cold such as a blade of grass or a window. White ice crystals form. We call this frost.

▽ Trees and plants look all white the morning after a frost.

◁On a freezing night, when cold air meets a cold window pane, it leaves patterns on the glass.

▷ When water vapour freezes onto twigs and spiders' webs, tiny crystals of ice grow. This is frost.

Freezing and thawing

In very cold weather the surface of the ground may freeze. If rain falls, it will freeze on the surface and form a layer of ice. Ice on the ground is very dangerous. It makes it difficult to walk or drive. Cars slide on the road. In icy weather water can freeze inside pipes. They need to be protected with cloths so that the water inside does not freeze.

▷ When the weather freezes and then thaws, it makes rocks split. This is what has caused the shape of these rocks.

▽ Many car accidents in winter are caused by ice on the road.

◁ If ice melts from a rooftop during the day, a cold night may freeze the drips into icicles.

▷ Water can freeze in pipes and make them burst. Water will flood everywhere when the ice thaws.

11

Blizzards

A heavy snowstorm with a wind blowing too is called a **blizzard**. Blizzards are dangerous because the temperature is freezing and it is difficult to see and move about. The wind blows snow into deep piles called **drifts**. Many people have jobs in which it is important to know whether blizzards are on their way, such as farmers.

▷ During a blizzard the wind blows down the snow like a white curtain.

▷ Drifting snow can bury farm animals. Farmers have to go and rescue the animals as they may die.

▷ Blizzards are dangerous for air travel. Planes may not be able to take off and runways have to be cleared.

Dangers of snow and ice

In the mountains, great masses of snow sometimes slide down the steep slopes. The falling snow buries everything in its path. This is an **avalanche** and it is very dangerous. Snow also causes other dangers. Drifts can block roads and cover signposts and road markings. People may lose their way and become stranded.

▷ Avalanches may start when the temperature rises and the snow begins to melt.

▽ Helicopters are used to rescue people who are stranded in the snow.

△ Snow makes everything look quite different. When it covers roads and signposts it is easy to lose the way. Vehicles can get stuck in drifting snow.

Clearing snow

Heavy falls of snow cause problems in towns and in the country. **Snowploughs** are used to clear roads and keep them open to traffic. If snow is forecast, lorries may sprinkle salt or grit on the roads. Salt helps to stop the snow from settling and freezing. The salt is mixed with grit to help car tyres grip the surface of the road.

▽ Snowploughs can help clear the roads of snow.

▷ Clearing snow from pathways makes it easier for people to get about.

▽ Roads are cleared of heavy snow, and salt and grit are sprinkled on the roads to help make them safer.

Snow and ice on land

Snow does not fall evenly around the world. Some places never have snow. Mountains often have snowy **peaks** all year round. This is because it is much colder on high ground. Ice and snow may wear away or change the shape of rocks. Freezing and thawing causes the rocks to crack or break. On mountains, rivers of ice called **glaciers** grind away at the rock and make deep valleys.

▷ The peak of this mountain is covered in snow. Plants grow on the lower slopes where it is much warmer.

▽ Glaciers are rivers of ice. They cut away at the mountain rock. Pieces of rock are carried along and left at the bottom of the slope.

A snowy world

At opposite ends of the earth are the North and South Poles. The area around the North Pole is called the Arctic. It is mainly frozen ocean. The area around the South Pole is called the Antarctic. They are the coldest places on earth. For much of the year the **polar lands** are frozen and the land is covered in snow and ice. In summer, most of the ice and snow thaws.

▽ In the Antarctic, almost all the land is covered with ice. Snow and ice are deeper here than anywhere else in the world.

North Pole
Arctic

South Pole
Antarctic

△ The polar lands lie
at the top and at the
bottom of the earth.

△ Here we can look
straight down at the
Arctic and the
Antarctic. They
cover the lands
coloured white.

Living with ice and snow

People who live in the ice and snow have learnt how to survive the harsh weather. Houses are built to keep in the warmth and not to fall down under the weight of the snow. People in the Arctic use snow mobiles to move around. They cross the ice more easily than using wheels. In other snowy places, people put chains on car wheels.

▽ In the Arctic, snow mobiles are used to get around.

▷ Houses in mountain areas have steep roofs to help the snow slide off.

▽ In places where it snows each winter, drivers put chains or special snow tyres on their cars to help grip the road.

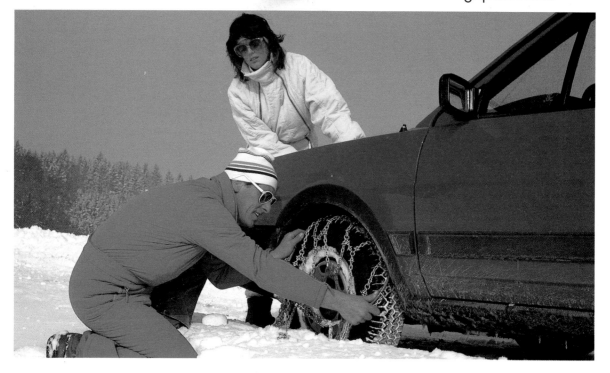

23

Plants of snow and ice

Plants which grow in places where there is a lot of snow and ice have to be able to survive cold, wind, and little rain. Most plants which grow in polar lands or high on mountains are small and lie low on the ground. **Conifer** trees grow in many snowy places. These trees have springy branches which bend under the weight of the snow.

▷ Conifer trees have branches which bend to stop them snapping under the heavy snow.

◁ Edelweiss grows in the mountains. It is covered in tiny hairs.

△ Crocus grow in early spring when there is still snow on the ground. They push through the snow to flower.

▷ Bearberry is a plant which grows in the Arctic. It is small and grows in clusters.

Animals of snow and ice

Many animals do not like cold and icy weather. The snow covers the plants they eat. Some birds **migrate**, or go to warmer places before the winter begins. Other animals **hibernate**, sleeping through the cold months. Animals in polar lands have thick coats to survive the cold. Some animals living in cold places turn white so that they cannot be easily seen against the snow.

▷ Polar bears have thick coats and large furry pads on their feet.

▽ The Arctic stoat and hare both turn white in winter. This hides them in the snow.

◁ Penguins have a thick layer of fat to keep warm. A chick is protected by sitting on the parent's feet and being covered.

▷ Swallows cannot survive the cold winter weather. They migrate to warmer places.

▽ When the ground is frozen, food is hard to find. Many birds rely on berries to survive.

◁ Chipmunks hibernate during the winter months.

Enjoying snow and ice

Would you like to live in the Arctic or the Antarctic? Many people dislike snow and ice because they cause so many problems.

If you dress warmly and are able to get about easily, snow can be a lot of fun. You can build snowmen with it and play all kinds of exciting games and sports.

▽ Cross-country skiing is popular in countries such as Norway, where there is much snow in winter.

▽ Toboggans slide easily across the snow. They travel downhill fast.

△ Snowmen are fun to build, but they disappear when it thaws.

◁ Ice hockey is a popular game in countries where it always snows in winter.

Things to do

- Try catching a snowflake. You will have to wait for it to snow before you can do this! Ask an adult if you can borrow a magnifying glass. Wrap up warmly to go outside, and make sure you have some gloves on. Catch snowflakes on your gloves and quickly look at the snowflake with the magnifying glass. Do all the snowflakes have the same pattern?

- When the earth becomes hard and icy, birds find it difficult to find food. Put some bread, nuts or scraps of cheese and bacon rind outside in the garden or on a window ledge. Watch how many different types of birds come to feed. You can make lists of which birds come each day.

Glossary

avalanche A large mass of loose snow which falls downhill.

blizzard A snowstorm where the wind is also blowing.

coast The area of land that is next to the sea.

conifer A tree which has cones and stays green all year round.

drifts Deep banks of snow which the wind has piled up.

equator An imaginary line around the middle of the earth.

freezing point The temperature at which a liquid or gas freezes. The freezing point of water is 0°C.

glacier A river of ice which moves slowly down a mountain or across land.

hibernate To spend the winter in a deep sleep-like state.

ice crystals Structures which are patterned and made from ice. They form as tiny water droplets freeze.

migrate To travel regularly from one part of the world to another in certain seasons of the year. Swallows migrate to cool countries in summer and to warm countries in winter.

peak The top of a mountain. Some peaks are pointed.

polar lands The area of land and sea around the North and South Poles.

snowplough A bulldozer-like vehicle which is fitted with a piece of equipment to clear snow out of the way.

temperature A kind of measurement that shows how hot or cold something is.

thaw To become warmer than freezing point and so begin to melt.

vapour Water in the form of a gas or very fine mist.

water cycle The endless pattern in which water, in the shape of rain, snow, or hail, falls, turns into a gas and rises, turning into droplets of water again, and falls once more.

water vapour An invisible gas in the air. Water becomes a gas when it dries out.

Index

King's Road Primary School
Rosyth - Tel: 313470

Photographic credits: B & C
Alexander 17, Bruce Coleman Ltd
(B Coleman) 7, (F de Nooyer) 8,
(F Eriza) 20, (T Buchhol) 28;
Robert Harding 11, 19,
(R Mcleod) 4; Hutchison Library
(B Regent) 3; ZEFA 13, 15, 23,
25, 27.